Grandma Abuela

Gammy Bube

Grand-mère

Seanmháthair Nai

Gram

Nanna Nonna

Gran Abuela

Grandma

Gammy Bube

Oma

Grand-mère

Seanmháthair

Gram

Nai Nanna Nonna

Gran Abuela

Grandma

Gammlemor

Gammy

Oma Grand-mè

Seanmháthair

Gram

Nai Nai Nanna

Gran

Nonna

Abuela Gammlemor

This Prayer Journal belongs to

....

Love from Grandma: A Prayer Journal

© 2008 Ellie Claire Gift & Paper Corp.

www.ellieclaire.com

Compiled by Barbara Farmer

Designed by Lisa & Jeff Franke

ISBN 978-1-934770-28-3

Printed in China

Love from Grandma

A PRAYER JOURNAL

gift & paper expressions

...inspired by life

My Grandchildren

Abigal Hardin   6-23-
GRANDCHILD   DATE OF BIRTH

Mark + Sue Hardin
            PARENTS

Trenton T. Hardin   12-25-
GRANDCHILD   DATE OF BIRTH

Mark + Sue Hardin
            PARENTS

GRANDCHILD   DATE OF BIRTH

PARENTS

GRANDCHILD   DATE OF BIRTH

PARENTS

GRANDCHILD   DATE OF BIRTH

PARENTS

Grandchildren are the dots that
connect the lines from
generation to generation.

Lois Wyse

My Grandchildren

Tyler Clasco Hardin   11-11-
GRANDCHILD   DATE OF BIRTH

Jeff + Cheri Hardin
PARENTS

Joshua T. Hardin   1-10-
GRANDCHILD   DATE OF BIRTH

Jeff + Cheri Hardin
PARENTS

GRANDCHILD   DATE OF BIRTH

PARENTS

GRANDCHILD   DATE OF BIRTH

PARENTS

GRANDCHILD   DATE OF BIRTH

PARENTS

It's such a grand thing to be a mother
of a mother—that's why the world
calls her grandmother.

My Grandchildren
(adopted)

Kelsey Lorene O'Brien   12-11-89
GRANDCHILD   DATE OF BIRTH

Sid & Cindy O'Brien
PARENTS

Connor Delbert O'Brien   3-23-
GRANDCHILD   DATE OF BIRTH

PARENTS

GRANDCHILD   DATE OF BIRTH

PARENTS

GRANDCHILD   DATE OF BIRTH

PARENTS

GRANDCHILD   DATE OF BIRTH

PARENTS

The neatest thing about Granny is that
every one of us was her favorite.

Salvation

Love is always free to love and arms are always
stretched as wide as the cross toward anyone
who needs to be loved.

Eugenia Price

Salvation

"I tell you the truth, you must accept the kingdom of God as if you were a little child, or you will never enter it." Then Jesus took the children in His arms, put His hands on them, and blessed them.

Mark 10:15–16 NCV

I pray You will touch the heart of each of my children...

Mark & Sue for Strength & guidance in all that they do.

Jeff & Cheri for Strength & guidance in all that they do raising their children

Sid & Cindy as they raise & guide their kids & for Strength & Courage

I pray You will touch the heart of each of my grandchildren...

- God, I Pray you will guide Abby in making right Choices & school and get her proper rest in her Body.

- Pray for Trent - guide his life & give him strength for each day. Help him as he plays sports and do his home work.

- Pray for Tyler - that he will make right choices & learn to love & respect his elders.

- The Same with little Joshua. Guide him & help him to be calm - mold him after your dear self

- for Kelsey - in all her college classes & help her to make good choices

- For Joshua Connor - help him in School & Work to make good Choices - may God use him mightily

Here's a special need I have today, God:

That my children will lean completely upon you + each of our grandchildren will learn to love + adore you as I do. Thank you Lord for your strength + courage to them each day. May each of them live their lives to the fullest for you.

HIGHLIGHT OF THE DAY
Praise and Thanksgiving

- When Joshua prayed + said grace at the dinner table tonite. He is only 5 yrs. old. — What a delight! They are so humble + direct when they pray + ask God for everything.

THOUGHT FOR THE DAY

Just as Jesus took the children, put His hands on them and blessed them...
we can hold our children in our arms, touching, blessing, and praying over them.

Quin Sherrer

Salvation

GOD'S WORD FOR ME TODAY

God our Savior...wants everyone to be saved and to understand the truth.
For there is only one God and one Mediator who can reconcile God
and humanity—the man Christ Jesus.

1 Timothy 2:3-5 NLT

I pray for spiritual understanding for my children...

....

....

....

....

....

....

I pray for spiritual understanding for my grandchildren...

....

....

....

....

....

....

....

Here's a special need I have today, God:

....

....

....

....

HIGHLIGHT OF THE DAY
Praise and Thanksgiving

....

....

....

....

....

....

THOUGHT FOR THE DAY

Heavenly Father, constantly remind me of the responsibility
I have to teach my children about You. Help me find ways throughout
the day to tell them of Your love, mercy and majesty. Amen.

Kim Boyce

Salvation

GOD'S WORD FOR ME TODAY

For God so loved the world that He gave His only begotten Son,
that whoever believes in Him should not perish but have everlasting life.

John 3:16 NLT

I pray for believing hearts for my children...

....

....

....

....

....

....

I pray for believing hearts for my grandchildren...

....

....

....

....

....

....

Here's a special need I have today, God:

....

....

....

....

HIGHLIGHT OF THE DAY
Praise and Thanksgiving

....

....

....

....

....

....

....

THOUGHT FOR THE DAY

The God who made your children will hear your petitions.
He has promised to do so. After all, He loves them more than you do.

James Dobson

Salvation

GOD'S WORD FOR ME TODAY

God's readiness to give and forgive is now public.
Salvation's available for everyone!

Titus 2:11 THE MESSAGE

I pray for salvation for my children...

....

....

....

....

....

....

I pray for salvation for my grandchildren...

....

....

....

....

....

....

Here's a special need I have today, God:

....

....

....

....

HIGHLIGHT OF THE DAY
Praise and Thanksgiving

....

....

....

....

....

THOUGHT FOR THE DAY

At the very heart of the universe is God's desire
to give and to forgive.

Salvation

You have this faith and love because of your hope, and what you hope
for is kept safe for you in heaven. You learned about this hope when
you heard the message about the truth, the Good News.

Colossians 1:5 NCV

I pray for strong faith for my children...

....

....

....

....

....

....

I pray for strong faith for my grandchildren...

....

....

....

....

....

....

Here's a special need I have today, God:

....

....

....

....

HIGHLIGHT OF THE DAY
Praise and Thanksgiving

....

....

....

....

....

....

....

THOUGHT FOR THE DAY

Nothing worth doing is completed in our lifetime; therefore we must be saved by hope. Nothing we do can be fully appreciated alone; therefore we must be saved by love. Nothing true or beautiful or good makes total sense in any context of history; therefore we are saved by faith.

Reinhold Niebuhr

Salvation

GOD'S WORD FOR ME TODAY

A man has a hundred sheep but one of the sheep gets lost.... If he finds it he is happier about that one sheep than about the ninety-nine.... In the same way, your Father in heaven does not want any of these little children to be lost.

Matthew 18:12–14 NCV

I pray for my children to be found by You...

....

....

....

....

....

....

I pray for my grandchildren to be found by You...

....

....

....

....

....

....

Here's a special need I have today, God:

....

....

....

....

HIGHLIGHT OF THE DAY
Praise and Thanksgiving

....

....

....

....

....

....

THOUGHT FOR THE DAY

There is no one so far lost that Jesus cannot find him
and cannot save him.

Andrew Murray

Salvation

GOD'S WORD FOR ME TODAY

Let the little children come to Me, and don't prevent them.
For of such is the Kingdom of Heaven.

Matthew 19:14 TLB

I pray for heavenly treasure for my children...

....

....

....

....

....

I pray for heavenly treasure for my grandchildren...

....

....

....

....

....

....

Here's a special need I have today, God:

....

....

....

....

HIGHLIGHT OF THE DAY
Praise and Thanksgiving

....

....

....

....

....

....

....

THOUGHT FOR THE DAY

A young child, a fresh, uncluttered mind, a world before him—
to what treasures will you lead him?

Gladys M. Hunt

Answers to Prayer

I learned a lot about the faithfulness of God from my grandmother....
She delighted in caring for me not because of anything I did,
but simply because I was hers.

Health and Safety

There is no safer place to be than
in the Father's hands.

Health and Safety

GOD'S WORD FOR ME TODAY

I pray that you may enjoy good health and that all may go well
with you, even as your soul is getting along well.

3 John 1:2 NIV

I pray for health and well-being for my children...

....

....

....

....

....

....

I pray for health and well-being for my grandchildren...

....

....

....

....

....

....

Here's a special need I have today, God:

....

....

....

....

HIGHLIGHT OF THE DAY
Praise and Thanksgiving

....

....

....

....

....

....

THOUGHT FOR THE DAY

I said a prayer for you today and I know God must have heard,
I felt the answer in my heart although He spoke no word.
I asked that He'd be near you at the start of each new day,
To grant you health and blessings and friends to share the way.

Health and Safety

GOD'S WORD FOR ME TODAY

I will cover you with My hands and protect you.

Isaiah 51:16 NCV

I pray for Your protection for my children...

....

....

....

....

....

....

I pray for Your protection for my grandchildren...

....

....

....

....

....

....

Here's a special need I have today, God:

....

....

....

....

....

Praise and Thanksgiving

....

....

....

....

....

....

....

THOUGHT FOR THE DAY

When you were small and just a touch away, I covered you with blankets
against the cool night air. But now that you are tall and out of reach,
I fold my hands and cover you with prayer.

Dona Maddux Cooper

Health and Safety

GOD'S WORD FOR ME TODAY

The eternal God is your Refuge.
And underneath are the everlasting arms.

Deuteronomy 33:27 TLB

I pray for Your loving, rescuing arms for my children...

....
....
....
....
....
....

I pray for Your loving, rescuing arms for my grandchildren...

....
....
....
....
....
....

Here's a special need I have today, God:

....

....

....

....

HIGHLIGHT OF THE DAY
Praise and Thanksgiving

....

....

....

....

....

....

....

THOUGHT FOR THE DAY

Whatever mistakes we may make, we shall come safely home. Slippings and strayings there will be, no doubt, but the everlasting arms are beneath us; we shall be caught, rescued, restored. This is God's promise; this is how good He is.

J. I. Packer

Health and Safety

God Himself is right alongside to keep you steady and on track....
God, who got you started in this spiritual adventure, shares with us
the life of His Son.... He will never give up on you.

1 Corinthians 1:8-9 THE MESSAGE

I pray for Your companionship for my children...

....
....
....
....
....

I pray for Your companionship for my grandchildren...

....
....
....
....
....

Here's a special need I have today, God:

....

....

....

....

HIGHLIGHT OF THE DAY
Praise and Thanksgiving

....

....

....

....

....

....

....

THOUGHT FOR THE DAY

Incredible as it may seem, God wants our companionship. He wants to
have us close to Him. He wants to be a father to us, to shield us, to protect us,
to counsel us, and to guide us in our way through life.

Billy Graham

Health and Safety

GOD'S WORD FOR ME TODAY

I will bring health and healing to the people there.
I will heal them and let them enjoy great peace and safety.

Jeremiah 33:6 NCV

I pray for health and healing for my children...

....

....

....

....

....

....

I pray for health and healing for my grandchildren...

....

....

....

....

....

....

Here's a special need I have today, God:

....

....

....

....

HIGHLIGHT OF THE DAY
Praise and Thanksgiving

....

....

....

....

....

....

....

THOUGHT FOR THE DAY

Beneath God's watchful eye His saints securely dwell;
That Hand which bears all nature up shall guard His children well.

William Cowper

Health and Safety

GOD'S WORD FOR ME TODAY

I urge you to pray for absolutely everything, ranging from small
to large. Include everything as you embrace this God-life,
and you'll get God's everything.

Mark 11:24 THE MESSAGE

I pray for confidence in Your help for my children...

....
....
....
....
....

I pray for confidence in Your help for my grandchildren...

....
....
....
....
....

Here's a special need I have today, God:

....
....
....
....

HIGHLIGHT OF THE DAY
Praise and Thanksgiving

....
....
....
....
....
....

THOUGHT FOR THE DAY

We sometimes fear to bring our troubles to God, because they must seem so small to Him who sitteth on the circle of the earth. But if they are large enough to vex and endanger our welfare, they are large enough to touch His heart of love.

Reuben A. Torrey

Health and Safety

I will lie down and sleep in peace, for You alone,
O Lord, make me dwell in safety.

Psalm 4:8 NIV

I pray for peace, no matter what, for my children...

....

....

....

....

....

....

I pray for peace, no matter what, for my grandchildren...

....

....

....

....

....

....

Here's a special need I have today, God:

....

....

....

....

....

....

....

....

....

....

....

THOUGHT FOR THE DAY

O heavenly Father, protect and bless all things that have breath:
guard them from all evil and let them sleep in peace.

Albert Schweitzer

Answers to Prayer

A grandmother is all those wonderful things
you never outgrow your need for.

Wisdom and Guidance

For the Lord gives wisdom, and from His mouth come knowledge and understanding.... He guards the course of the just and protects the way of His faithful ones.

Proverbs 2:6, 8 NLT

Wisdom and Guidance

GOD'S WORD FOR ME TODAY

What a God we have!... We've been given a brand-new life and have
everything to live for, including a future in heaven—and the future starts now!
God is keeping careful watch over us and the future.

1 Peter 1:3–5 THE MESSAGE

I pray for wisdom for my children...

....

....

....

....

....

....

I pray for wisdom for my grandchildren...

....

....

....

....

....

....

....

Here's a special need I have today, God:

....

....

....

....

....

HIGHLIGHT OF THE DAY
Praise and Thanksgiving

....

....

....

....

....

....

....

THOUGHT FOR THE DAY

This bright, new day, complete with 24 hours of opportunities, choices,
and attitudes comes with a perfectly matched set of 1440 minutes.
This unique gift, this one day, cannot be exchanged, replaced or refunded.
Handle with care. Make the most of it. There is only one to a customer!

Wisdom and Guidance

GOD'S WORD FOR ME TODAY

Wise choices will watch over you.
Understanding will keep you safe.

Proverbs 2:11 NLT

I pray for spiritual understanding for my children...

....

....

....

....

....

....

I pray for spiritual understanding for my grandchildren...

....

....

....

....

....

....

Here's a special need I have today, God:

....

....

....

....

HIGHLIGHT OF THE DAY
Praise and Thanksgiving

....

....

....

....

....

....

THOUGHT FOR THE DAY

Choices can change our lives profoundly. The choice to mend a broken
relationship, to say "yes" to a difficult assignment, to lay aside some
important work to play with a child, to visit some forgotten person—
these small choices may affect many lives eternally.

Gloria Gaither

Wisdom and Guidance

GOD'S WORD FOR ME TODAY

God has given each of you some special abilities; be sure to use them to
help each other, passing on to others God's many kinds of blessings.

1 Peter 4:10 TLB

I pray my children have loving attitudes toward others...

....
....
....
....
....
....

I pray my grandchildren have loving attitudes toward others...

....
....
....
....
....
....

Here's a special need I have today, God:

....

....

....

....

HIGHLIGHT OF THE DAY
Praise and Thanksgiving

....

....

....

....

....

....

THOUGHT FOR THE DAY

How you do something and the attitude with which you do it are usually
even more important than what you do.... Often we have no choice
about doing things, but we can always choose how to do them.
And that...can make all the difference in your daily life.

Norman Vincent Peale

Wisdom and Guidance

GOD'S WORD FOR ME TODAY

He leads me beside the still waters. He restores my soul;
He leads me in the paths of righteousness for His name's sake.

Psalm 23:2–3 NKJV

I pray my children find and follow Your path...

....

....

....

....

....

....

I pray my grandchildren find and follow Your path...

....

....

....

....

....

....

Here's a special need I have today, God:

....

....

....

....

HIGHLIGHT OF THE DAY
Praise and Thanksgiving

....

....

....

....

....

....

....

THOUGHT FOR THE DAY

A new path lies before us; we're not sure where it leads;
But God goes on before us, providing all our needs.
This path, so new, so different; exciting as we climb;
Will guide us in His perfect will until the end of time.

Linda Maurice

Wisdom and Guidance

GOD'S WORD FOR ME TODAY

My child, don't lose sight of common sense and discernment. Hang on
to them, for they will refresh your soul. They are like jewels on a necklace.
They keep you safe on your way, and your feet will not stumble.

Proverbs 3:21–23 NLT

I pray my children seek spiritual discernment...

....

....

....

....

....

....

I pray my grandchildren seek spiritual discernment...

....

....

....

....

....

....

Here's a special need I have today, God:

....

....

....

....

HIGHLIGHT OF THE DAY
Praise and Thanksgiving

....

....

....

....

....

....

....

THOUGHT FOR THE DAY

Divine guidance is promised to us, and our faith must therefore
confidently look for and expect it.

Hannah Whitall Smith

Wisdom and Guidance

GOD'S WORD FOR ME TODAY

I am the Lord your God, who teaches you what is good for you
and leads you along the paths you should follow.

Isaiah 48:17 NLT

I pray my children have teachable hearts...

....

....

....

....

....

....

I pray my grandchildren have teachable hearts...

....

....

....

....

....

....

Here's a special need I have today, God:

....

....

....

....

....

HIGHLIGHT OF THE DAY
Praise and Thanksgiving

....

....

....

....

....

....

....

THOUGHT FOR THE DAY

Heaven often seems distant and unknown, but if He who made the road...
is our guide, we need not fear to lose the way.

Henry Van Dyke

Wisdom and Guidance

GOD'S WORD FOR ME TODAY

O Lord, You are our Father; We are the clay, and You our potter;
And all we are the work of Your hand.

Isaiah 64:8 NKJV

I pray You will guide my influence on my children...

....

....

....

....

....

....

I pray You will guide my influence on my grandchildren...

....

....

....

....

....

....

Here's a special need I have today, God:

....
....
....
....

HIGHLIGHT OF THE DAY
Praise and Thanksgiving

....
....
....
....
....
....

THOUGHT FOR THE DAY

Oh God, You have given me a vacant soul, an untaught conscience,
a life of clay. Put Your big hands around mine and guide my hands so
that every time I make a mark on this life, it will be Your mark.

Gloria Gaither

Answers to Prayer

[Grandma] was a very special person to talk to. Sometimes,
she would give you the right answers without ever saying a word.

Harry McMahan

....

....

....

....

....

....

....

....

....

....

....

....

....

....

....

....

....

....

Gifts and Purpose

For we are God's masterpiece.
He has created us anew in Christ Jesus,
so we can do the good things
He planned for us long ago.

Ephesians 2:10 NLT

Gifts and Purpose

GOD'S WORD FOR ME TODAY

You are the light of the world. A city that is set on a hill cannot be hidden....
Let your light so shine before men, that they may see your good works
and glorify your Father in heaven.

Matthew 5:14, 16 NKJV

I pray for my children to shine Your light...

....
....
....
....
....
....

I pray for my grandchildren to shine Your light...

....
....
....
....
....
....

Here's a special need I have today, God:

....

....

....

....

....

HIGHLIGHT OF THE DAY
Praise and Thanksgiving

....

....

....

....

....

....

....

THOUGHT FOR THE DAY

One person, like one candle in a dark room...like one pebble tossed
into the water...like one word spoken at the perfect time....
One person called by God can make a difference in the world.

Gifts and Purpose

GOD'S WORD FOR ME TODAY

Go after a life of love as if your life depended on it—because it does.
Give yourselves to the gifts God gives you.

1 Corinthians 14:1-2 THE MESSAGE

I pray my children find and use their spiritual gifts...

....

....

....

....

....

....

I pray my grandchildren find and use their spiritual gifts...

....

....

....

....

....

....

Here's a special need I have today, God:

....

....

....

....

HIGHLIGHT OF THE DAY
Praise and Thanksgiving

....

....

....

....

....

....

....

THOUGHT FOR THE DAY

Remember that you are needed. There is at least one important work
to be done that will not be done unless you do it.

Charles Allen

Gifts and Purpose

GOD'S WORD FOR ME TODAY

There are different kinds of gifts, but they are all from the same Spirit.
There are different ways to serve but the same Lord to serve....
God works in all of us in everything we do. Something from the Spirit
can be seen in each person, for the common good.

1 Corinthians 12:4–7 NCV

I pray my children have confidence in their gifts...

....

....

....

....

....

I pray my grandchildren have confidence in their gifts...

....

....

....

....

....

Here's a special need I have today, God:

....

....

....

....

....

HIGHLIGHT OF THE DAY
Praise and Thanksgiving

....

....

....

....

....

....

....

THOUGHT FOR THE DAY

No one else has been gifted by God exactly like you. There is a place in our family that is yours alone. No one else has your talents, your abilities, your set of strengths to bring to that place. God designed you for it...you are a perfect fit.

Gifts and Purpose

GOD'S WORD FOR ME TODAY

We constantly pray for you, that our God may count you worthy of
His calling, and that by His power He may fulfill every good purpose
of yours and every act prompted by your faith.

2 Thessalonians 1:11 NIV

I pray for a worthy purpose for my children...

....

....

....

....

....

....

I pray for a worthy purpose for my grandchildren...

....

....

....

....

....

....

Here's a special need I have today, God:

....

....

....

....

....

HIGHLIGHT OF THE DAY

Praise and Thanksgiving

....

....

....

....

....

....

....

THOUGHT FOR THE DAY

Many persons have a wrong idea of what constitutes real happiness. It is not obtained through self-gratification, but through fidelity to a worthy purpose.

Helen Keller

Gifts and Purpose

GOD'S WORD FOR ME TODAY

For Christ's love compels us.... And He died for all, that those who live should no longer live for themselves but for Him who died for them and was raised again.

2 Corinthians 5:14-15 NIV

I pray Your love motivates my children...

....
....
....
....
....
....

I pray Your love motivates my grandchildren...

....
....
....
....
....
....

Here's a special need I have today, God:

....

....

....

....

HIGHLIGHT OF THE DAY
Praise and Thanksgiving

....

....

....

....

....

....

....

THOUGHT FOR THE DAY

Recognizing who we are in Christ and aligning our life with God's purpose
for us gives a sense of destiny.... It gives form and direction to our life.

Jean Fleming

Gifts and Purpose

GOD'S WORD FOR ME TODAY

We know that all things work together for good to those who love God,
to those who are the called according to His purpose.

Romans 8:28 NKJV

I pray my children see Your purpose in them...

....
....
....
....
....
....

I pray my grandchildren see Your purpose in them...

....
....
....
....
....
....

Here's a special need I have today, God:

_____
_____
_____
_____

HIGHLIGHT OF THE DAY
Praise and Thanksgiving

_____
_____
_____
_____
_____
_____

THOUGHT FOR THE DAY

When we allow God the privilege of shaping our lives, we discover new depths of purpose and meaning. What a joyful thought to realize you are a chosen vessel for God—perfectly suited for His use.

Joni Eareckson Tada

Gifts and Purpose

GOD'S WORD FOR ME TODAY

Well done, good and faithful servant! You have been faithful
with a few things; I will put you in charge of many things.
Come and share your master's happiness!

Matthew 25:21 NIV

I pray my children serve You faithfully...

....

....

....

....

....

....

I pray my grandchildren serve You faithfully...

....

....

....

....

....

....

Here's a special need I have today, God:

....

....

....

....

....

....

....

....

....

....

....

THOUGHT FOR THE DAY

Not everyone possesses boundless energy or a conspicuous talent.
We are not equally blessed with great intellect or physical beauty or emotional
strength. But we have all been given the same ability to be faithful.

Gigi Graham Tchividjian

Answers to Prayer

There is no better gift I can give my grandchildren than to show them
how to keep a quiet heart in this loud and busy world.

....

....

....

....

....

....

....

....

....

....

....

....

....

....

....

....

....

....

Friends

Friends warm you with their presence,
trust you with their secrets,
and remember you in their prayers.

Friends

GOD'S WORD FOR ME TODAY

The sweet smell of perfume and oils is pleasant,
and so is good advice from a friend.

Proverbs 27:9 NCV

I pray my children know how to trust and be trustworthy...

....

....

....

....

....

....

I pray my grandchildren know how to trust and be trustworthy...

....

....

....

....

....

....

Here's a special need I have today, God:

....

....

....

....

HIGHLIGHT OF THE DAY
Praise and Thanksgiving

....

....

....

....

....

....

....

THOUGHT FOR THE DAY

What a blessing is a friend with a heart so trustworthy that you may safely bury all your secrets in it,...who can relieve your cares by her words, your doubts by her advice, your sadness by her good humor, and whose very look gives comfort to you.

Friends

GOD'S WORD FOR ME TODAY

Love one another the way I loved you.
This is the very best way to love.

John 15:12 THE MESSAGE

I pray for brotherly love for my children...

....

....

....

....

....

I pray for brotherly love for my grandchildren...

....

....

....

....

....

....

Here's a special need I have today, God:

....

....

....

....

....

HIGHLIGHT OF THE DAY
Praise and Thanksgiving

....

....

....

....

....

....

....

THOUGHT FOR THE DAY

Friends remind us we are part of something greater than ourselves,
a larger world, and the right friends keep us on track.

Barbara Jenkins

Friends

I always thank my God as I remember you in my prayers, because I hear
about your faith in the Lord Jesus and your love for all the saints.

Philemon 1:4–5 NIV

I pray my children will wisely choose their friends...

....

....

....

....

....

....

I pray my grandchildren will wisely choose their friends...

....

....

....

....

....

....

Here's a special need I have today, God:

....

....

....

....

....

HIGHLIGHT OF THE DAY
Praise and Thanksgiving

....

....

....

....

....

....

....

THOUGHT FOR THE DAY

True happiness consists not in the multitude of friends,
but in the worth and choice.

Ben Jonson

Friends

GOD'S WORD FOR ME TODAY

A friend is always loyal, and a brother is born
to help in time of need.

Proverbs 17:17 NLT

I pray for loyal friends for my children...

....
....
....
....
....

I pray for loyal friends for my grandchildren...

....
....
....
....
....

Here's a special need I have today, God:

....

....

....

....

HIGHLIGHT OF THE DAY
Praise and Thanksgiving

....

....

....

....

....

....

....

THOUGHT FOR THE DAY

True friendships are lasting because true love is eternal. A friendship in which heart speaks to heart is a gift from God, and no gift that comes from God is temporary or occasional. All that comes from God participates in God's eternal life.

Henri J. M. Nouwen

Friends

Above all, clothe yourselves with love, which binds us all
together in perfect harmony.

Colossians 3:14 NLT

I pray my children find a best friend for life...

....

....

....

....

....

....

I pray my grandchildren find a best friend for life...

....

....

....

....

....

Here's a special need I have today, God:

....

....

....

....

....

HIGHLIGHT OF THE DAY
Praise and Thanksgiving

....

....

....

....

....

....

....

THOUGHT FOR THE DAY

The gift of friendship—both given and received—is joy, love and nurturing
for the heart. The realization that you have met a soul mate...a kindred spirit...
a true friend...is one of life's sweetest gifts!

Friends

GOD'S WORD FOR ME TODAY

The right word at the right time is like a custom-made piece of jewelry,
And a wise friend's timely reprimand is like a gold ring slipped on your finger.

Proverbs 25:11–12 THE MESSAGE

I pray for praying friends for my children...

....

....

....

....

....

I pray for praying friends for my grandchildren...

....

....

....

....

....

Here's a special need I have today, God:

....

....

....

....

HIGHLIGHT OF THE DAY
Praise and Thanksgiving

....

....

....

....

....

....

....

THOUGHT FOR THE DAY

Friends are an indispensable part of a meaningful life. They are the ones who share
our burdens and multiply our blessings.... In good times and bad, we need friends who
will pray for us, listen to us, and lend a comforting hand and an understanding ear.

Beverly LaHaye

Friends

Greater love has no one than this, than to
lay down one's life for his friends.

John 15:13 NKJV

I pray my children's friends will draw them closer to You...

....

....

....

....

....

....

I pray my grandchildren's friends will draw them closer to You...

....

....

....

....

....

....

Here's a special need I have today, God:

....

....

....

....

....

HIGHLIGHT OF THE DAY
Praise and Thanksgiving

....

....

....

....

....

....

....

THOUGHT FOR THE DAY

Dare to love and to be a real friend. The love you give and receive
is a reality that will lead you closer and closer to God as well as
to those whom God has given you to love.

Henri J. M. Nouwen

Answers to Prayer

The closest friends I have made all through life have been people who also grew up close to a loved and loving grandmother.

Margaret Mead

....

....

....

....

....

....

....

....

....

....

....

....

....

....

....

....

....

....

....

....

A Love of a Lifetime

Marriage is the beautiful
blending of two lives,
two loves,
two hearts.
It's the wonderful mystical moment
when a beautiful love story starts.

A Love of a Lifetime

GOD'S WORD FOR ME TODAY

If you love someone you will be loyal to him...you will always believe in him,
always expect the best of him, and always stand your ground in defending him.

1 Corinthians 13:7 TLB

I pray my children will be and seek a godly spouse...

....
....
....
....
....
....

I pray my grandchildren will be and seek a godly spouse...

....
....
....
....
....
....
....

Here's a special need I have today, God:

....

....

....

....

HIGHLIGHT OF THE DAY
Praise and Thanksgiving

....

....

....

....

....

....

THOUGHT FOR THE DAY

A happy and successful marriage comes not so much from finding
the right partner, but rather from being the right partner and
demonstrating love, faith, hope, and forgiveness.

A Love of a Lifetime

GOD'S WORD FOR ME TODAY

If two lie down together, they will keep warm....
Though one may be overpowered, two can defend themselves.
A cord of three strands is not quickly broken.

Ecclesiastes 4:11–12 NIV

I pray for my children too be equally yoked in You...

....

....

....

....

....

....

I pray for my grandchildren too be equally yoked in You...

....

....

....

....

....

....

Here's a special need I have today, God:

....

....

....

....

....

HIGHLIGHT OF THE DAY
Praise and Thanksgiving

....

....

....

....

....

....

THOUGHT FOR THE DAY

It takes three persons to make a satisfying marriage. A husband, a wife, and God.
Marriage can be a beautiful, deeply satisfying, fulfilling relationship.
But only because God is in it.

Jack and Carol Mayhall

A Love of a Lifetime

GOD'S WORD FOR ME TODAY

Love each other...and take delight in honoring each other.

Romans 12:10 TLB

I pray my children find romance in their marriage...

....

....

....

....

....

....

....

I pray my grandchildren find romance in their marriage...

....

....

....

....

....

....

....

Here's a special need I have today, God:

....
....
....
....
....

HIGHLIGHT OF THE DAY
Praise and Thanksgiving

....
....
....
....
....
....
....

THOUGHT FOR THE DAY

Romance is eager—striving always to appear attractive to each other.
Love is two people who find beauty in each other—no matter how they look.

Marjorie Holmes

A Love of a Lifetime

GOD'S WORD FOR ME TODAY

Love flashes like fire, the brightest kind of flame.
Many waters cannot quench love, nor can rivers drown it.

Song of Solomon 8:6–7 NLT

I pray for true love for my children...

....

....

....

....

....

....

I pray for true love for my grandchildren...

....

....

....

....

....

....

Here's a special need I have today, God:

....

....

....

....

....

HIGHLIGHT OF THE DAY
Praise and Thanksgiving

....

....

....

....

....

....

....

THOUGHT FOR THE DAY

I think true love is never blind but rather brings an added light,
An inner vision quick to find the beauties hid from common sight.

Phoebe Cary

A Love of a Lifetime

GOD'S WORD FOR ME TODAY

Love never gives up. Love cares more for others than for self.
Love doesn't want what it doesn't have.

1 Corinthians 13:4 THE MESSAGE

I pray for selfless love for my children...

....

....

....

....

....

....

I pray for selfless love for my grandchildren...

....

....

....

....

....

....

Here's a special need I have today, God:

....

....

....

....

....

HIGHLIGHT OF THE DAY
Praise and Thanksgiving

....

....

....

....

....

....

....

THOUGHT FOR THE DAY

Love is not getting, but giving.... It is goodness and honor and peace
and pure living—yes, love is that and it is the best thing in the world
and the thing that lives the longest.

Henry Van Dyke

A Love of a Lifetime

GOD'S WORD FOR ME TODAY

When we love each other God lives in us and His love
within us grows ever stronger.

1 John 4:12 TLB

I pray for spiritual protection for my children's marriages...

....

....

....

....

....

....

I pray for spiritual protection for my grandchildren's marriages...

....

....

....

....

....

....

Here's a special need I have today, God:

....

....

....

....

HIGHLIGHT OF THE DAY
Praise and Thanksgiving

....

....

....

....

....

....

....

THOUGHT FOR THE DAY

There is nothing nobler or more admirable than when two people who
see eye to eye keep house as man and wife, confounding their enemies
and delighting their friends.

Homer

A Love of a Lifetime

GOD'S WORD FOR ME TODAY

May the Lord make your love increase and overflow for each other.

1 Thessalonians 3:12 NIV

I pray my children experience lifelong marriage...

....

....

....

....

....

....

I pray my grandchildren experience lifelong marriage...

....

....

....

....

....

....

Here's a special need I have today, God:

....

....

....

....

HIGHLIGHT OF THE DAY
Praise and Thanksgiving

....

....

....

....

....

....

THOUGHT FOR THE DAY

Love grows from our capacity to give what is deepest within ourselves and
also receive what is the deepest within another person. The heart becomes
an ocean strong and deep, launching all on its tide.

Answers to Prayer

There's no way to measure the value of a praying Grandmother.
Prayer is one of the richest gifts a grandchild can receive.

....

....

....

....

....

....

....

....

....

....

....

....

....

....

....

....

....

....

....

Fruits of the Spirit

The fruit of the Spirit is love, joy, peace, patience, kindness, goodness, faithfulness, gentleness and self-control.

Galatians 5:22–23 NIV

Fruits of the Spirit

GOD'S WORD FOR ME TODAY

So, chosen by God for this new life of love, dress in the wardrobe God picked out for you: compassion, kindness, humility, quiet strength, discipline. Be even-tempered, content with second place, quick to forgive an offense.

Colossians 3:12-13 THE MESSAGE

I pray for my children to dress in Your righteousness...

_____

_____

_____

_____

_____

_____

I pray for my grandchildren to dress in Your righteousness...

_____

_____

_____

_____

_____

_____

Here's a special need I have today, God:

....

....

....

....

....

HIGHLIGHT OF THE DAY

Praise and Thanksgiving

....

....

....

....

....

....

....

THOUGHT FOR THE DAY

Lord, give me an open heart to find You everywhere, to glimpse the heaven
enfolded in a bud, and to experience eternity in the smallest act of love.

Mother Teresa

Fruits of the Spirit

Let us consider how we may spur one another on
toward love and good deeds.

Hebrews 10:24 NIV

I pray for kindness and courtesy in my children...

....

....

....

....

....

....

I pray for kindness and courtesy in my grandchildren...

....

....

....

....

....

....

Here's a special need I have today, God:

....

....

....

....

HIGHLIGHT OF THE DAY
Praise and Thanksgiving

....

....

....

....

....

....

....

THOUGHT FOR THE DAY

A good deed is never lost; he who sows courtesy reaps friendship,
and he who plants kindness gathers love.

Basil

Fruits of the Spirit

GOD'S WORD FOR ME TODAY

A generous man will prosper; he who refreshes others
will himself be refreshed.

Proverbs 11:25 NIV

I pray for a generous heart within my children...

I pray for a generous heart within my grandchildren...

Here's a special need I have today, God:

....

....

....

....

HIGHLIGHT OF THE DAY
Praise and Thanksgiving

....

....

....

....

....

....

....

THOUGHT FOR THE DAY

I expect to pass through life but once. If therefore, there can be any kindness
I can show, or any good thing I can do to any fellow being, let me do it now...
as I shall not pass this way again.

William Penn

Fruits of the Spirit

GOD'S WORD FOR ME TODAY

When God lives and breathes in you..., you are delivered from that dead life.
With His Spirit living in you, your body will be as alive as Christ's!

Romans 8:11 THE MESSAGE

I pray for my children to be alive in You...

....

....

....

....

....

I pray for my grandchildren to be alive in You...

....

....

....

....

....

Here's a special need I have today, God:

....

....

....

....

HIGHLIGHT OF THE DAY
Praise and Thanksgiving

....

....

....

....

....

....

....

THOUGHT FOR THE DAY

Life is what we are alive to. It is not length but breadth.... Be alive to...goodness, kindness, purity, love, history, poetry, music, flowers, stars, God, and eternal hope.

Maltbie D. Babcock

Fruits of the Spirit

GOD'S WORD FOR ME TODAY

Since we are living by the Spirit, let us follow the Spirit's
leading in every part of our lives.

Galatians 5:25 NLT

I pray for love in every part of my children's lives...

....

....

....

....

....

....

I pray for love in every part of my grandchildren's lives...

....

....

....

....

....

....

Here's a special need I have today, God:

....

....

....

....

HIGHLIGHT OF THE DAY
Praise and Thanksgiving

....

....

....

....

....

....

....

THOUGHT FOR THE DAY

Joy is love exalted; peace is love in repose; long-suffering is love enduring;
gentleness is love in society; goodness is love in action; faith is love on the
battlefield; meekness is love in school; and temperance is love in training.

Dwight L. Moody

Fruits of the Spirit

GOD'S WORD FOR ME TODAY

Walk with Me and work with Me—watch how I do it. Learn the unforced
rhythms of grace. I won't lay anything heavy or ill-fitting on you.
Keep company with Me and you'll learn to live freely and lightly.

Matthew 11:29-30 THE MESSAGE

I pray for spiritual dependence on You for my children...

....

....

....

....

....

....

I pray for spiritual dependence on You for my grandchildren...

....

....

....

....

....

....

Here's a special need I have today, God:

....

....

....

....

....

HIGHLIGHT OF THE DAY
Praise and Thanksgiving

....

....

....

....

....

....

....

THOUGHT FOR THE DAY

Love comes while we rest against our Father's chest.
Joy comes when we catch the rhythms of His heart.
Peace comes when we live in harmony with those rhythms.

Ken Gire

Fruits of the Spirit

GOD'S WORD FOR ME TODAY

Pray in the Spirit on all occasions with all kinds of prayers and requests.
With this in mind, be alert and always keep on praying for all the saints.

Ephesians 6:18 NIV

I pray for my children to seek the fruits of the Spirit...

....

....

....

....

....

....

I pray for my grandchildren to seek the fruits of the Spirit...

....

....

....

....

....

....

Here's a special need I have today, God:

....

....

....

....

....

HIGHLIGHT OF THE DAY
Praise and Thanksgiving

....

....

....

....

....

....

....

THOUGHT FOR THE DAY

To pray is to change. This is a great grace. How good of God to provide a path
whereby our lives can be taken over by love and joy and peace and patience
and kindness and goodness and faithfulness and gentleness and self-control.

Richard J. Foster

Answers to Prayer

Grandmothers are a gift of grace. In God's masterful design, grandmothers encircle us with love and weave heavenly roses into our lives.

....

....

....

....

....

....

....

....

....

....

....

....

....

....

....

....

....

....

....

....

Family Relationships

Family faces are magic mirrors.
Looking at people who belong to us,
we see the past, present, and future.

Gail Lumet Buckley

Family Relationships

GOD'S WORD FOR ME TODAY

I will sing of the mercies of the Lord forever; with my mouth
will I make known Your faithfulness to all generations.

Psalm 89:1 NKJV

I pray for a spiritually connected family for my children...

....

....

....

....

....

....

I pray for a spiritually connected family for my grandchildren...

....

....

....

....

....

....

Here's a special need I have today, God:

....

....

....

....

....

HIGHLIGHT OF THE DAY
Praise and Thanksgiving

....

....

....

....

....

....

THOUGHT FOR THE DAY

A genuine faith is like a golden thread that joins the hearts of
one generation to the hearts of another.

Roy Lessin

Family Relationships

GOD'S WORD FOR ME TODAY

May your roots go down deep into the soil of God's marvelous love;
and may you be able to feel and understand...how long, how wide,
how deep, and how high His love really is.

Ephesians 3:17–18 TLB

I pray for familial stability for my children...

....

....

....

....

....

....

I pray for familial stability for my grandchildren...

....

....

....

....

....

....

Here's a special need I have today, God:

....

....

....

....

....

HIGHLIGHT OF THE DAY
Praise and Thanksgiving

....

....

....

....

....

....

....

THOUGHT FOR THE DAY

To be rooted is perhaps the most important and
least recognized need of the human soul.

Simone Weil

Family Relationships

Your word, O Lord, is eternal; it stands firm in the heavens.
Your faithfulness continues through all generations.

Psalm 119:89–90 NIV

I pray my children enjoy and pass on our family traditions...

....

....

....

....

....

....

....

I pray my grandchildren enjoy and pass on our family traditions...

....

....

....

....

....

....

....

Here's a special need I have today, God:

....

....

....

....

....

HIGHLIGHT OF THE DAY
Praise and Thanksgiving

....

....

....

....

....

....

THOUGHT FOR THE DAY

Tradition gives us a sense of solidarity and roots, a knowing there
are some things one can count on.

Gloria Gaither

Family Relationships

Regarding life together and getting along with each other, you don't need me to tell you what to do. You're God-taught in these matters. Just love one another!

1 Thessalonians 4:9 THE MESSAGE

I pray for peaceful coexistence for my children...

....

....

....

....

....

I pray for peaceful coexistence for my grandchildren...

....

....

....

....

....

....

Here's a special need I have today, God:

....

....

....

....

....

HIGHLIGHT OF THE DAY
Praise and Thanksgiving

....

....

....

....

....

....

THOUGHT FOR THE DAY

You don't choose your family. They are God's gift to you,
as you are to them.

Desmond Tutu

Family Relationships

GOD'S WORD FOR ME TODAY

God decided in advance to adopt us into His own family by
bringing us to Himself through Jesus Christ. This is what
He wanted to do, and it gave Him great pleasure.

Ephesians 1:5 NLT

I pray for nurturing family love for my children...

....

....

....

....

....

....

I pray for nurturing family love for my grandchildren...

....

....

....

....

....

....

Here's a special need I have today, God:

....
....
....
....

HIGHLIGHT OF THE DAY
Praise and Thanksgiving

....
....
....
....
....
....
....

THOUGHT FOR THE DAY

A strong sense of family unity, belonging, and warmth doesn't just happen.
It is nurtured and grown over time, just as a lovely garden flourishes
in the hands of a caring, diligent gardener.

Richard Patterson Jr.

Family Relationships

We, Your people and sheep of Your pasture, will give You thanks forever;
we will show forth Your praise to all generations.

Psalm 79:13 NKJV

I pray for my children's future generation...

....

....

....

....

....

....

I pray for my grandchildren's future generation...

....

....

....

....

....

....

Here's a special need I have today, God:

....

....

....

....

....

HIGHLIGHT OF THE DAY
Praise and Thanksgiving

....

....

....

....

....

....

....

THOUGHT FOR THE DAY

We close our eyes, we bow our heads and offer thanks for daily bread....
And our children shall sit with their own children small,
And give thanks, once again, for the miracle of it all.

Steve Myrvang

Family Relationships

GOD'S WORD FOR ME TODAY

Come, you children, listen to me;
I will teach you the fear of the Lord.

Psalm 34:11 NKJV

I pray for a praying family for my children...

....

....

....

....

....

I pray for a praying family for my grandchildren...

....

....

....

....

....

Here's a special need I have today, God:

....

....

....

....

HIGHLIGHT OF THE DAY
Praise and Thanksgiving

....

....

....

....

....

....

....

THOUGHT FOR THE DAY

Prayers arising out of the context of the family are perhaps the most
common expression of praying.... As we pray in the context of the family,
we learn that holiness is homemade.

Richard J. Foster

Answers to Prayer

There's no place like home—except Grandma's.

....

....

....

....

....

....

....

....

....

....

....

....

....

....

....

....

Trusting God

The more we depend on God the more
dependable we find He is.

Sir Cliff Richard

Trusting God

GOD'S WORD FOR ME TODAY

High above the sky, or in the deepest ocean—nothing will ever
be able to separate us from the love of God.

Romans 8:39 TLB

I pray my children understand how much You love them...

....

....

....

....

....

....

I pray my grandchildren understand how much You love them...

....

....

....

....

....

....

Here's a special need I have today, God:

....

....

....

....

....

HIGHLIGHT OF THE DAY
Praise and Thanksgiving

....

....

....

....

....

....

....

THOUGHT FOR THE DAY

God loves and cares for us, even to the least event
and smallest need of life.

Henry Edward Manning

Trusting God

God's way is perfect. All the Lord's promises prove true.
He is a shield for all who look to Him for protection.

Psalm 18:30 NLT

I pray my children rely on Your timing...

....
....
....
....
....
....

I pray my grandchildren rely on Your timing...

....
....
....
....
....
....

Here's a special need I have today, God:

....

....

....

....

HIGHLIGHT OF THE DAY
Praise and Thanksgiving

....

....

....

....

....

....

THOUGHT FOR THE DAY

God's timing is rarely our timing. But far better than we do, He numbers
our days and knows our moments and our hours. Our task is to trust.

Os Guinness

Trusting God

Our soul waits for the Lord; He is our help and our shield. For our heart shall rejoice in Him, because we have trusted in His holy name.

Psalm 33:20-21 NKJV

I pray my children will fully trust in You...

....

....

....

....

....

....

I pray my grandchildren will fully trust in You...

....

....

....

....

....

....

Here's a special need I have today, God:

....

....

....

....

HIGHLIGHT OF THE DAY
Praise and Thanksgiving

....

....

....

....

....

....

THOUGHT FOR THE DAY

God will never, never, never let us down if we have faith and put our
trust in Him. He will always look after us. So we must cleave to Jesus.
Our whole life must simply be woven into Jesus.

Mother Teresa

Trusting God

I love the Lord because He hears my prayers and answers them.
Because He bends down and listens, I will pray as long as I breathe!

Psalm 116:1–2 TLB

I pray my children will know that they are heard...

....
....
....
....
....
....

I pray my grandchildren will know that they are heard...

....
....
....
....
....
....

Here's a special need I have today, God:

....

....

....

....

....

HIGHLIGHT OF THE DAY
Praise and Thanksgiving

....

....

....

....

....

....

....

THOUGHT FOR THE DAY

So wait before the Lord. Wait in the stillness. And in that stillness, assurance will come to you. You will know that you are heard;...you will hear quiet words spoken to you yourself, perhaps to your grateful surprise and refreshment.

Amy Carmichael

Trusting God

Cast all your anxiety on Him because He cares for you.

1 Peter 5:7

I pray my children will cast all their cares upon You...

....

....

....

....

....

....

I pray my grandchildren will cast all their cares upon You...

....

....

....

....

....

....

Here's a special need I have today, God:

....

....

....

....

....

HIGHLIGHT OF THE DAY
Praise and Thanksgiving

....

....

....

....

....

....

THOUGHT FOR THE DAY

Because God is responsible for our welfare, we are told to cast all our care upon Him, for He cares for us. God says, "I'll take the burden—don't give it a thought—leave it to Me."

Billy Graham

Trusting God

You will keep in perfect peace all who trust in You, all whose thoughts are fixed
on You! Trust in the Lord always, for the Lord God is the eternal Rock.

Isaiah 26:3-4 NLT

I pray my children rest in faith upon Your greatness...

....

....

....

....

....

....

I pray my grandchildren rest in faith upon Your greatness...

....

....

....

....

....

....

Here's a special need I have today, God:

....

....

....

....

....

....

....

....

....

....

....

THOUGHT FOR THE DAY

God is looking for people who will come in simple dependence
upon His grace, and rest in simple faith upon His greatness.
At this very moment, He's looking at you.

Jack Hayford

Trusting God

GOD'S WORD FOR ME TODAY

For all God's words are right, and everything He does is worthy of our trust.
He loves whatever is just and good; the earth is filled with His tender love.

Psalm 33:4-5 TLB

I pray my children know You are as good as Your word...

....

....

....

....

....

....

I pray my grandchildren know You are as good as Your word...

....

....

....

....

....

....

Here's a special need I have today, God:

....

....

....

....

....

HIGHLIGHT OF THE DAY
Praise and Thanksgiving

....

....

....

....

....

....

....

THOUGHT FOR THE DAY

We may...depend upon God's promises, for...He will be as good as His word.
He is so kind that He cannot deceive us, so true that He cannot break His promise.

Matthew Henry

Answers to Prayer

I thank God, Grandma, for the blessing you are...for the joy of your laughter...
the comfort of your prayers...the warmth of your smile.

....

....

....

....

....

....

....

....

....

....

....

....

....

....

....

....

Hopes and Dreams

God is not too great to be concerned
about our smallest wishes.

Basilea Schlink

Hopes and Dreams

GOD'S WORD FOR ME TODAY

My heart is confident in You, O God; my heart is confident.
No wonder I can sing Your praises!

Psalm 57:7 NLT

I pray my children are confident in Your leading...

....

....

....

....

....

....

I pray my grandchildren are confident in Your leading...

....

....

....

....

....

....

Here's a special need I have today, God:

....

....

....

....

....

HIGHLIGHT OF THE DAY
Praise and Thanksgiving

....

....

....

....

....

....

THOUGHT FOR THE DAY

Go confidently in the direction of your dreams! Live the life you've imagined.
As you simplify your life, the laws of the universe will be simpler.

Henry David Thoreau

Hopes and Dreams

GOD'S WORD FOR ME TODAY

We continually remember before our God and Father your work
produced by faith, your labor prompted by love, and your endurance
inspired by hope in our Lord Jesus Christ.

1 Thessalonians 1:3 NIV

I pray for inspiration for my children...

....

....

....

....

....

....

I pray for inspiration for my grandchildren...

....

....

....

....

....

....

Here's a special need I have today, God:

....

....

....

....

....

HIGHLIGHT OF THE DAY
Praise and Thanksgiving

....

....

....

....

....

....

....

THOUGHT FOR THE DAY

When you are inspired by a dream, God has hit the ball into your court.
Now you have to hit it back with commitment.

Robert Schuller

Hopes and Dreams

GOD'S WORD FOR ME TODAY

I pray that God, the source of hope, will fill you completely with joy and peace because you trust in Him. Then you will overflow with confident hope through the power of the Holy Spirit.

Romans 15:13 NLT

I pray You will be the source of hope for my children...

....

....

....

....

....

I pray You will be the source of hope for my grandchildren...

....

....

....

....

....

....

Here's a special need I have today, God:

....

....

....

....

HIGHLIGHT OF THE DAY
Praise and Thanksgiving

....

....

....

....

....

....

THOUGHT FOR THE DAY

Do not pray for dreams equal to your powers.
Pray for powers equal to your dreams.

Adelaide Anne Procter

Hopes and Dreams

Trust in the Lord with all your heart, and lean not on your own understanding;
in all your ways acknowledge Him, and He shall direct your paths.

Proverbs 3:5–6 NKJV

I pray for God-given dreams for my children...

....

....

....

....

....

....

I pray for God-given dreams for my grandchildren...

....

....

....

....

....

....

Here's a special need I have today, God:

....

....

....

....

....

HIGHLIGHT OF THE DAY
Praise and Thanksgiving

....

....

....

....

....

....

....

THOUGHT FOR THE DAY

Allow your dreams a place in your prayers and plans. God-given dreams
can help you move into the future He is preparing for you.

Barbara Johnson

Hopes and Dreams

GOD'S WORD FOR ME TODAY

Souls who follow their hearts thrive.

Proverbs 13:19 THE MESSAGE

I pray my children will follow their dreams...

....

....

....

....

....

....

I pray my grandchildren will follow their dreams...

....

....

....

....

....

....

Here's a special need I have today, God:

....

....

....

....

HIGHLIGHT OF THE DAY
Praise and Thanksgiving

....

....

....

....

....

....

....

THOUGHT FOR THE DAY

At every crossroad, follow your dream. It is courageous
to let your heart lead the way.

Thomas Leland

Hopes and Dreams

GOD'S WORD FOR ME TODAY

Many people will praise God because you obey the Good News
of Christ—the gospel you say you believe—and because
you freely share with them and with all others.

2 Corinthians 9:13 NCV

I pray my children will lead others to You...

_____

_____

_____

_____

_____

_____

I pray my grandchildren will lead others to You...

_____

_____

_____

_____

_____

_____

Here's a special need I have today, God:

....

....

....

....

HIGHLIGHT OF THE DAY
Praise and Thanksgiving

....

....

....

....

....

....

....

THOUGHT FOR THE DAY

She who wishes to secure the good of others
has already secured her own.

Hopes and Dreams

GOD'S WORD FOR ME TODAY

Two people are better than one, because they
get more done by working together.

Ecclesiastes 4:9 NCV

I pray for encouragement from others for my children...

....

....

....

....

....

....

I pray for encouragement from others for my grandchildren...

....

....

....

....

....

....

Here's a special need I have today, God:

....

....

....

....

HIGHLIGHT OF THE DAY
Praise and Thanksgiving

....

....

....

....

....

....

....

THOUGHT FOR THE DAY

When we dream alone it remains only a dream. When we dream together,
it is not just a dream. It is the beginning of reality.

Dom Helder Camara

Answers to Prayer

Grandma always made you feel she had been waiting to see
just you all day and now the day was complete.

Marcy DeMaree

....

....

....

....

....

....

....

....

....

....

....

....

....

....

....

Education and Career

Every day we live is a priceless gift of God,
loaded with possibilities to learn
something new, to gain fresh insights.

Dale Evans Rogers

Education and Career

GOD'S WORD FOR ME TODAY

Many, O Lord my God, are Your wonderful works which You
have done; and Your thoughts toward us cannot be recounted...
they are more than can be numbered.

Psalm 40:5 NKJV

I pray my children desire a lifetime of learning...

....

....

....

....

....

I pray my grandchildren desire a lifetime of learning...

....

....

....

....

....

Here's a special need I have today, God:

....

....

....

....

HIGHLIGHT OF THE DAY
Praise and Thanksgiving

....

....

....

....

....

....

THOUGHT FOR THE DAY

Whether sixty or sixteen, there is in every human being's heart the love of
wonder, the sweet amazement at the stars and starlike things, the undaunted
challenge of events, the unfailing childlike appetite for what-next,
and the joy of the game of living.

Samuel Ullman

Education and Career

GOD'S WORD FOR ME TODAY

I will praise You, for I am fearfully and wonderfully made;
marvelous are Your works, and that my soul knows very well.

Psalm 139:14 NKJV

I pray for diligence in studying for my children...

....
....
....
....
....
....

I pray for diligence in studying for my grandchildren...

....
....
....
....
....
....
....

Here's a special need I have today, God:

....

....

....

....

....

HIGHLIGHT OF THE DAY
Praise and Thanksgiving

....

....

....

....

....

....

....

THOUGHT FOR THE DAY

My business is not to remake myself, but to make
the absolute best of what God made.

Robert Browning

Education and Career

GOD'S WORD FOR ME TODAY

You will enjoy what you work for, and you
will be blessed with good things.

Psalm 128:2 NCV

I pray my children will appreciate hard work...

....

....

....

....

....

....

I pray my grandchildren will appreciate hard work...

....

....

....

....

....

....

Here's a special need I have today, God:

....

....

....

....

HIGHLIGHT OF THE DAY
Praise and Thanksgiving

....

....

....

....

....

....

THOUGHT FOR THE DAY

All work, from the simplest chore to the most challenging and complex undertaking, is a wonder and a miracle. It is a gift and a blessing that God has given us.... To work is to do something essential to our humanness.

Ben Patterson

Education and Career

Whatever you do, work at it with all your heart,
as working for the Lord, not for men.

Colossians 3:23 NIV

I pray my children find adventure in their work...

....

....

....

....

....

....

I pray my grandchildren find adventure in their work...

....

....

....

....

....

....

Here's a special need I have today, God:

....

....

....

....

....

HIGHLIGHT OF THE DAY
Praise and Thanksgiving

....

....

....

....

....

....

....

THOUGHT FOR THE DAY

Go forth seeking adventure. Open your eyes, your ears, your mind,
your heart, your spirit and you'll find adventure everywhere.... It is in your
daily work.... Think of whatever you are doing as an adventure and
watch your life change for the better.

Wilferd A. Peterson

Education and Career

Wise words bring many benefits,
and hard work brings rewards.

Proverbs 12:14 NLT

I pray my children find great rewards in their work...

....
....
....
....
....
....

I pray my grandchildren find great rewards in their work...

....
....
....
....
....
....

Here's a special need I have today, God:

....

....

....

....

HIGHLIGHT OF THE DAY
Praise and Thanksgiving

....

....

....

....

....

....

....

THOUGHT FOR THE DAY

Far and away the best prize that life offers is the chance
to work hard at work worth doing.

Theodore Roosevelt

Education and Career

GOD'S WORD FOR ME TODAY

Let the beauty of the Lord our God be upon us, and establish the
work of our hands for us; yes, establish the work of our hands.

Psalm 90:17 NKJV

I pray my children excel in their work...

....

....

....

....

....

....

I pray my grandchildren excel in their work...

....

....

....

....

....

....

Here's a special need I have today, God:

....

....

....

....

....

HIGHLIGHT OF THE DAY
Praise and Thanksgiving

....

....

....

....

....

....

THOUGHT FOR THE DAY

How do I love God?... By doing beautifully the work I have been
given to do, by doing simply that which God has entrusted to me,
in whatever form it may take.

Mother Teresa

Education and Career

GOD'S WORD FOR ME TODAY

God can do anything, you know—far more than you could ever imagine or guess or request in your wildest dreams! He does it not by pushing us around but by working within us, His Spirit deeply and gently within us.

Ephesians 3:20 THE MESSAGE

I pray my children are grateful for their work...

....

....

....

....

....

....

I pray my grandchildren are grateful for their work...

....

....

....

....

....

....

....

Here's a special need I have today, God:

....

....

....

....

HIGHLIGHT OF THE DAY
Praise and Thanksgiving

....

....

....

....

....

....

....

THOUGHT FOR THE DAY

Nothing enters your life accidentally—remember that.
Behind our every experience is our loving, sovereign God.

Charles R Swindoll

Answers to Prayer

A grandmother can be one of the most important
teachers a child ever has.

....

....

....

....

....

....

....

....

....

....

....

....

....

....

....

....

....

....

....

....

Future Plans and Blessings

God puts each fresh morning,
each new chance of life,
into our hands as a gift to see
what we will do with it.

Future Plans and Blessings

GOD'S WORD FOR ME TODAY

Grace and peace be given to you more and more, because you truly
know God and Jesus our Lord. Jesus has the power of God, by which
He has given us everything we need to live and to serve God.

2 Peter 1:2-3 NCV

I pray for Your spiritual blessing upon my children...

....

....

....

....

....

....

I pray for Your spiritual blessing upon my grandchildren...

....

....

....

....

....

....

Here's a special need I have today, God:

....

....

....

....

....

HIGHLIGHT OF THE DAY
Praise and Thanksgiving

....

....

....

....

....

....

....

THOUGHT FOR THE DAY

Have you ever thought that in every action of grace in your heart
you have the whole omnipotence of God engaged to bless you?

Andrew Murray

Future Plans and Blessings

GOD'S WORD FOR ME TODAY

Beloved, let us love one another, for love is of God;
and everyone who loves is born of God and knows God.

1 John 4:7 NKJV

I pray my children desire to know You more...

....
....
....
....
....
....

I pray my grandchildren desire to know You more...

....
....
....
....
....
....

Here's a special need I have today, God:

....

....

....

....

....

HIGHLIGHT OF THE DAY
Praise and Thanksgiving

....

....

....

....

....

....

THOUGHT FOR THE DAY

What makes life worthwhile is having a big enough objective, something which catches our imagination and lays hold of our allegiance.... What higher, more exalted, and more compelling goal can there be than to know God?

J. I. Packer

Future Plans and Blessings

GOD'S WORD FOR ME TODAY

"For I know the plans I have for you," declares the Lord, "plans to prosper
you and not to harm you, plans to give you hope and a future."

Jeremiah 29:11 NIV

I pray my children find joy in living the life You gave them...

....
....
....
....
....
....

I pray my grandchildren find joy in living the life You gave them...

....
....
....
....
....
....

Here's a special need I have today, God:

....

....

....

....

....

....

....

....

....

....

....

THOUGHT FOR THE DAY

We have been...designed with a unique, one-of-a-kind soul that exists forever—
whether we live it as a burden or a joy...doesn't change the fact that
we've been given the gift of *being* now and forever.... We are handcrafted
by God, who has a personal design and plan for each of us.

Future Plans and Blessings

GOD'S WORD FOR ME TODAY

Pursue righteous living, faithfulness, love, and peace. Enjoy the companionship of those who call on the Lord with pure hearts.

2 Timothy 2:22 NLT

I pray for all Your blessings for my children...

....

....

....

....

....

....

I pray for all Your blessings for my grandchildren...

....

....

....

....

....

....

Here's a special need I have today, God:

....

....

....

....

....

HIGHLIGHT OF THE DAY
Praise and Thanksgiving

....

....

....

....

....

....

....

THOUGHT FOR THE DAY

I wish you love, and strength, and faith, and wisdom, goods, gold enough
to help some needy one. I wish you songs, but also blessed silence,
and God's sweet peace when every day is done.

Dorothy Nell McDonald

Answers to Prayer

Nothing gives me greater joy than to hear that my
children are following the way of truth.

3 John 1:4 NCV
